BRIAN WHITTINGHAM, born and liv
fiction writer, editor and creative
tions include *Drink the Green Fairy* and *The Old Man From Brooklyn*
and the Charing Cross Carpet. Recent plays include *Smugglers and
Black-Damp* and *The Devil's Dandruff.* In 1994 Brian was awarded a
month's fellowship in Yaddo artists' colony in Saratoga Springs, New
York where he co-wrote *Diamonds in Bedlam* with Glasgow songwriter,
Willie Black, which they performed during the *Birth of Impressionism*
Exhibition in Glasgow. In 2000 he won first prize in the *Sunday Herald*
Short Story Competition. His poems and stories have been widely pub-
lished in anthologies and magazines. A former steelworker/draughtsman,
he performed his steelworking poems as part of the BBC's 'Ballad of
the Big Ships Live' at Glasgow's Royal Concert Hall in 2007. He has
performed and lectured in the UK, Europe and the USA, in places as
diverse as beaches, universities, prisons, pubs, schools and colleges.
He is currently a lecturer in creative writing at Glasgow's College of
Nautical Studies.

By the Same Author

Drink the Green Fairy 2004
Septimus Pitt and the Grumbleoids 2007
*Clocking In Clocking Out: Poems and Photographs
on the Subject of Work* 2012

Bunnets n Bowlers

A Clydeside Odyssey

BRIAN WHITTINGHAM

Luath Press Limited

EDINBURGH

www.luath.co.uk

*Dedicated to all who have ever worked
with the Black Squad*

First published 2009
Reprinted 2009
Reprinted 2010
Reprinted 2015

ISBN: 978-1-906307-94-3

The publishers acknowledge the support of

Scottish
Arts Council

towards the publication of this volume.

The paper used in this book is recyclable. It is made from
low-chlorine pulps produced in a low energy, low emissions manner
from renewable forests.

Printed and bound by
Bell & Bain Ltd., Glasgow

Typeset in 11 point Sabon
by 3btype.com

All images except on page 10 courtesy of
The Herald & Evening Times picture archive.

Contents

Foreword

THE ATLANTIC LUXURY LINERS, the *Lusitania*, the *Aquitania*, the *Queen Mary*, the *Queen Elizabeth* and the QE2, were built by the shipyard workers at John Brown's in Clydebank.

All these ships had stories attached to them, stories of bowler hats, the foremen whose job it was to make sure deadlines were met, and stories of bunnets, the skilled artisans that honed, shaped and formed the steel to the instructions supplied by the thousands of blueprints that resulted in the completed Ocean-going liner.

One such liner was the QE2 and this collection of poetry is my Clydeside odyssey from when I left school at 15, working for a year as an office boy then serving a four year apprenticeship as a boilermaker's plater, then becoming a journeyman plater, much of the time working on the QE2.

Queen Elizabeth 2 (HULL NO 736) 1967

The last great trans-Atlantic liner to be built on the Clyde.

By October 1961 Cunard realised the highly successful Queens could not be repeated, because the need for an all year round weekly Atlantic service had gone.[1] Jet aeroplanes had become the fast way for the wealthy to cross the Atlantic and luxury shipping lines had to find new ways of filling their ships. When Cunard launched the QE2 in 1967, they offered new style sailings across the Atlantic and winter holiday cruises around the Caribbean. These cruises successfully attracted a broader market

---

[1]   *Cunard press release 4 April 1967*

to sample life aboard a luxury liner and turned around Cunard's trading losses.

The QE2 was launched from its grease laden slipway at 2.28pm on 20 September 1967. And as a 17-year-old apprentice I was among the cheering 30,000 soaking up the excitement of the big day. The next day would be a return to the mundane with a 7.30am start, a 10 hour day working in the fabrication shed with a Baltic wind blowing off the Clyde, punctuated only by breaks where the typical repast would be cheese pieces and boiling cans of tea. So an official day off work, with bands and the air full of excitement, was a welcome change.

Little did I know that 40 years later at 2.28pm on 20 September 2007 I would be sitting on board the QE2, docked for the day in Greenock, in the Mauritania Restaurant with Craig, my 24-year-old son, at a reception lunch sipping Cabernet Sauvignon and dining on Medallions of Spring Lamb, Wild Mushroom Fricassee, Armagnac Macerated Apricots and Lavender Jus with Rosti Potato.

Looking at the menu with the legend, 40 *Years Famous*, I remembered the words spoken earlier as we sipped our complimentary champagne while we were welcomed on board by the MD of the Cunard Line. She said that she (the QE2) had come home to her own, as if the liner belonged to the workers who built her. I felt it ironic that few of us would ever have been able to afford the fare that would let us have a taste of the luxury on offer.

Then my interest strayed to the photograph on the menu. It showed the almost completed liner resting on the slipway in the background and in the foreground, a group of boilersuited players kicking a ball about during dinner time football. My mind jumped to past games, kicking a plastic ball with steel toe-capped boots, and while I pondered on these thoughts, a white gloved waiter refilled my wine glass, then ever so delicately brushed the crumbs off the white linen tablecloth.

For 40 years the images that were branded into my psyche have been floating about in my head and for the past 20 years I've been writing poems about my time in John Brown's with memories periodically surfacing on an ongoing basis. The poems contained within are a result of this journey I've taken. Of course, it's been punctuated with many other journeys as all our lives are, but for me this has been special in forming who I am today. This was brought home to me recently when I went to the site of the shipyard which is now just a piece of flattened land. It's as if nothing had happened there at all, as if any traces of its previous existence had been erased. All that's left is a TITAN crane that tourists can now ascend so they can get a bird's eye view of the shipyard that's no longer there.

So this collection is more than just reminisces, it is a social diary of lives, attitudes and an environment that reflects the many working class communities that no longer exist. Communities that never again will be.

It's strange to think that 40 years after working in the yard I was to be one of the guests invited on board when the QE2 docked in at Greenock on its last voyage round the UK. I was lucky enough to have my son with me so I could share a part of me when I was a teenager. Our photograph is shown in this book – one that I'm very proud of. We still debate who is the taller between us. Friendly teasing. And for all the fondness there is in the relationship, I'm glad he didn't follow in my footsteps by working in the yards. I wouldn't wish that kind of work on anyone. While we ex-workers reminisce and joke about the good old days, the grim reality was quite different as perhaps you'll discover yourself when you read these poems. Welcome to what was once my world!

The Office Boy

Filed index card
after index card
after index card
after index card.

Made tea and, sometimes, coffee
as and when he was told.

Delivered plans and files
and memos and faxes
to very important people.

Played dinner time
shove ha'penny
with animated skill.

Watched the men
in a circle six deep
playing pitch and toss.

Listened to the exploits
of drinkers and shaggers,
dancers and chancers.

Dreamed of becoming
a marine engineer
with a girl in every port

and sat beside an old rate-fixer
who kept telling the boy
to stop dreaming because
he'd turn out like him in with the bricks
and the nearest he would get to sea
was watching Popeye on the TV
and what a pleasure it would be
to have a bowl of the secretary's bathwater
for a plate of soup
on a cold winter's evening.

The Rookie

was a smart-arsed apprentice
who gave the men lip

and didn't realise it was his job
to be told what to do
no matter what

until

a self-appointed committee
persuaded him to enter the boiler room
where they pinned him to the floor,
pulled down his trousers,
smeared his balls with axle grease,
waste oil and wood chippings
all the time
muttering pleasantries about his manhood.

The rookie had a lot to learn.

The Apprentice

In the freezing cold shed

Wearing brand new overalls
miles too big.
Humphing angle-bars
that dug into your shoulders.
Marking off plates
with a hammer and dab.
Hitting your fingers
getting blood-black nails.
Drinking red-hot tea.
Eating three cheese chits
in ten minutes.
Learning to weld.
Getting a flash in your eye.
Getting dirty nippy tears.

Being gallus at the buff
not wearing any goggles
and screwing up your eyes
giving the sparks a smaller target
while you ground down your fingers a bit.

Playing dinner time football
showing your skills
running over railway lines swerving the ball
with your steel-toe capped boots,
kicking it in the dock,
going in the rowing boat to get it
hoping you got back in time
for the twelve-thirty-seven whistle.

Working the big press
Hoping you didn't end up with nine fingers
Like your mate who would kid on
He was picking his nose
With his missing digit.
Listening to journeymen
always talking about their nookie,
Especially Sam Abbott
The knicker knocker from Duntocher.

Sweeping rusty plates.
Working the pyramid rolls
hoping the menacing rolled metal
wouldn't fall on your napper.
Putting the plate-lifters in
and watching the shoogly mass
swinging way above your head.
Shouting and bawling
and making signs to the crane man.
Listening to caulkers
giving you a bit of the old industrial deafness.

Going home clatty and knackered
and being told

'So long as you've got a trade behind you son.'

Message in a Bottle

Fifteen-year-old office boy,
dinner time,
(no one called it lunch)
walking through the yard
across glinting railway lines
towards the ship
to see what it looked like
from underneath the hull
that could crush
if it had the inclination.

Passing
       rusty hills of drag chain.
Passing
       sturdy timber stocks
       like thickly clustered tree trunks.
Passing
       men seated on toolbox lids
       drinking cans of steaming tea.
Passing
       dancing flames heating noisy conversation
       that ruffled the coldness in the air.

Feeling the chill
in the mind
in the steel

and going down to the river's edge
with rusted welding rods
and spearing bobbing bottles.

One breaks
releasing a piece of paper
with a message written
in a language I couldn't understand.

The Health Hazards of Alcohol

Sitting in the boilermaker's club
drinking like men
talking like men
eyeing the women like men

with our fully paid-up union cards
in our hips
and our four-year apprenticeships behind us

and I could handle anything
until Sammy Johnstone,
who, incidentally, was one crazy guy,
reminded me
that if I didn't bring in a bottle of whisky
the next day he would
'Kick fuck' out of me,
and Clattie Wattie
who was a Blue-Angel[1],
put me at ease
saying he would rearrange Sammy's face
with his now empty tumbler

---

[1] *the Blue-Angels – A motorcycle gang*

Wattie obviously forgot
about the time
Sammy was bevvied
and hit Tim McLauchlin over the head
with his two-and-a-half-pound hammer
because he didn't like Catholics

and the violent cabaret
rollercoastered my insides
and I went home that night
and cried.

At the Furnace

At the tea-break
the caulker
lit the pointed corners
of the upside-down paper poke.

The seated audience
of platers and burners
and welders and riggers
and labourers and apprentices
applauded,
stood and saluted,
as they watched it float
high in the shed
like a hot-air balloon
with the lightness of feathers
but without the beauty.

Dead Man's Hand

Wild Bill Hickok,
the welders' shop steward,
told of how he was shot from behind
while playing poker in Deadwood.

'My two pair of eights and aces
became known as "dead man's hand",'
he told his fellow boilermakers.

In the funnel-shop he'd wear his
bootlace-tie and black shirt
under his droopy Wild Bill mustache

and with his ceegar stuck to his bottom lip,
he'd spin a two-and-a-half-pound hammer
round his extended forefinger,
cock the trigger by brushing the palm
of his other hand
over the hammer's ball-peen,
and once he'd shot yet another foreman in the back,
he'd blow imaginary smoke
from the end of his
gun barrel hammer shaft.

When welding,
he would be showered by crackling sparks
enveloping his masked head
filled with Grand Ole Opry dreams
of cowgirls, hoedowns and Colt .45s

and of his trusty steed Trigger
that he rode on the Loch Lomond hills
on the rare occasion
he had a weekend off.

Remember

There was Jackie Liddle
        the shop steward with nine fingers
        who was collecting ten bob a head
        for the UCS work-in
        which was fair enough
        till we found out that
        Jackie had distribution problems
        after that
        he was known as Jackie Fiddle.

Then there was Irish Pat
        the burner who liked his bevvy too much
        so after dinner time you didn't ask him
        to do your job in the afternoon
        because it was like a dog pissing in the snow
        and he'd stay after stopping time
        and paint your toolbox inside and out for free
        killing time and probably himself
        till the nearest boozer opened at five.

Then there was Gunner
      the old sweeper-up who liked the Rolling Stones
      and would look at you with his glass eye
      puffing on his clay pipe
      leaning on his brush handle
      and tell you of the time
      the sheds in the yards had no roofs
      and you had to sweep the snow
      off the plates before your early morning start.

And then there was old Alex Easdale
      the plater with the shaky bunnet
      who used to be some kind of boxer
      who could still duck and jab
      with his timing not quite right
      and he kept his doups in his bunnet
      till his punch-drunk head shook once too much
      and his bunnet got caught in the buff
      and rather than have the shame
      of not having a bunnet he went out at dinner time
      and bought a brand spanking new one.

The Loftsman

taught his apprentice
to mark off burning templates.

Pens filled with Indian ink.
The young man carefully drew
the straight lines
on the white template paper
then with his compasses
his corner arcs
ensuring that when the lines merged
there were no smudges or splodges

because he was well aware
that if the template's outline
wasn't perfect,
the loftsman
would knuckle his fingers
and give the young man a sharp punch
on his arm muscle
again
and again
and again

leaving a mark
the young man
would never be able to get rid of.

The Old Man in the Tool-chest

that looked like a metal walk-in wardrobe
had decorated its interior
with home-from-home comforts.

A cushioned swivel chair.
A shelf for sly cans of tea.
and a locked cabinet for his half-bottle.

The base – floored with an off-cut
Paisley patterned lounge carpet.

The walls – covered with pouting,
licking girls, seductively stroking,
eyes only for him.

In between fabricating sections of ducting
he'd take impromptu breaks
when he'd hide inside his tool-chest
out of sight of the foreman.

He'd sit on his swivel chair
steal sips from his half-bottle of Grouse.
Peek through the slit in his
partially opened doors

and when any suit from the drawing office
invaded his territory
with plans and technical talk
about the latest piece of machinery
he'd quickly close his tool-chest door

and would shout out as loud as possible:

'You push switch A,
pull lever B,
and – if it's completely fucked!
you press the big red button.'

and smile to himself
taking another nip from his half-bottle,
satisfied he'd once again
taken on the smart-arsed designer
who minced about in his collar and tie
thinking he was the bee's knees.

Giving it Laldy in the Seven Seas

Outside the Seven Seas public bar,
the frosted windows
with etched illustrations of big ships
their sails, masts, rigging and deck-hands
battling crashing waves and thundering foam.

Inside the Seven Seas,
the bar staff lined up
quarter gills on the gantry
in preparation for the dinner time rush
of thirsty artisans
and quickly learning apprentices who would
have their liquid lunch
of goldies with half pint chasers.

In the evenings
sometimes, after another bout of overtime,
they would again congregate,
this time for a session of serious swallying
which, one evening, culminated in the apprentices
having a table-top tap-dancing competition
with the artisans giving it laldy singing
'Show me the Way to go Home!'

Signals

Finger tap on the wrist
asking for the time.

Flat horizontal hand across the throat,
answering
a quarter past the hour.

Rotating fist
with extended finger pointing skywards
telling the craneman
to raise his straining load.

Cupped hand under left nipple
showing far off figures
what they really are.

Balled rag in pocket pulled tight
showing imagined manhood.

Forefinger and thumb
plucking the air asking for a chalk line

and head nods to the right
indicating one more ...

... turn on the angle bender
... extra inch on the pyramid rolls
... pound of pressure on the hydraulic press

in a galvanised shed
surrounded by four walls of mayhem.

Spotted Hats

The welders wore spotted hats
of many different colours,
crude leather leggings,
aprons
and soft leather mitts.

They lit their wacky baccy
off glowing ends of hot electrodes

and would only consider maintenance
when their cables
sparked or smouldered or smoked.

And when they weren't bevvied

they would artistically
weld pipes with bevelled preps
and tackle 'overhead'
with a sureness of skill,

molten showers of sparks
pot-holing leathered protection
as they twisted their rods
to the most acute angles.

They viewed green glowing arcs
as low hydrogen fumes
snaked
round spacemen-like masks

and the slag on the weld
curled up like the tail of a scorpion.

Tommy Two-Thou

The inspector wore green overalls,
yellow hard hat
and carried a black clipboard.

He would hang over the side of the deck

a trapeze artist, eyeballing
his measuring tape
to ensure tolerances were adhered to.

On the ground he would
check vertical alignment
with his theodolite
like a surveyor on Mars.

And on finding the upper deck
to be one inch off the plumb,
Tommy Two-thou
would smile,
twitch his neck,
and stamp yet another inspection report failure.

Spinning Tea-Cans

A burner screwed up unprotected eyes
burning a white hot line
sometimes near dab marks
as spitting metal played roulette with his sight.

The plater placed his teeth
on a cracked porcelain basin
washing his grime-etched face
with cold water and Swarfega.

The press with the faulty pressure gauge
groaned and hissed its resistance
as the eight-fingered operator
ignited apprentice fear with his cackle.

The fledgling apprentice
filled his tea–can with boiling water,
learning to spin his arms like windmill blades
as he walked to his blustery toolbox seat

Quality Counts

The plate shop workers
always griped that because of

lousy designs and plans that were never clear

it was no wonder
the stainless steel units
ended up with sharp edges and gaps
that you could poke your head through

and with loopy delivery dates
that could never be met
and totally impractical piecework rates
and a crazy management
that now expected the men to work
right up to stopping time

it was inevitable the quality produced
by these skilled artisans
would be well below par

unless someone required
a made-to-measure wrought iron gate,
with accompanying made-to-measure
wrought iron fencing for their garden

then extremely accurate tolerances
a finish of the highest quality
and immediate delivery
would be the standing order of the day.

In the plate shed
the boilermakers understood
the importance of a homer – no question.

Assembly Line Hysteria

The press operator
sniffles the oil-cold air
drifting past his machine
like a cartoon aroma
as he looks at the open shed door.

The press operator
paints the thick oil
over the flatbar pipe-clips,
toughened steel ready for
the forming die in the press.

The press operator
places the flatbar
against backstops, instinctively
counteracts his sliding feet
on the oily timber walkway.

The press operator
strains the machine's lever
with his half–finger,
listening for the pitch of sound
that tells him
what the pressure gauge should.

The press operator
removes his formed pipe-clip
then re-oils the die.
He racks the pipe-clip
and re-oils the next piece of flatbar.

The press operator
sniffles the oil-cold air.

Swiss Watches and the Ballroom Dancer

The ballroom dancer
always wore
a white shirt under clean overalls.

He kept his bow tie for out of work.

In the boiler-shop
he waved his oxyacetylene heating torch
like a magic wand
the blue flame whooshing
over the edge of the upturned metal cone.

He hammered the red-hot metal
with his wooden mallet
that made him look like Thor, the god of thunder.

His flared edges
had a professional finish – no dents.

Gunner, he was on the same job,
didn't particularly care
if he deformed the metal's edge,
if he dented it or scraped it
as he battered it with his ball-peen hammer.

His flared edges
were patterned with gashes and dents.

'He thinks we're making Swiss watches…'
shouted Gunner into the air
as he observed the ballroom dancer

who cocked his left eye,
then demonstrated to his apprentice,
by gliding between two toolboxes,
how he would slide a leg
into his partner's groin
when doing the Paso Doble.

The Black Squad

In trap five, a welder
with his trousers hauled down
dozed, as his forehead rested
on crossed arms that lay on his knees.

In trap one, a plater
rustled a newspaper
and listened to the two-thirty from Aintree
in the cubicle with the best radio reception.

In trap two, a labourer
with DTs and a final warning
sat upright on his porcelain throne
accompanied by the hiss of a lager ring-pull.

In trap three, a greenhorn apprentice
tried hard to ignore the mirror
held, angled, at the top of his stall
that he kept closed by pushing his feet against the door.

In trap four, a caulker
read the graffiti that informed him
he was now doing a shit
at an angle of forty-five degrees.

And under a cracked wash-hand basin
a burner slouched while
studying page three nipples that he would add
to the gallery pinned above his oxygen bottles.

Daylight

The welder smoked his roll-up,
dragged his early morning cable
to his dockside welding pot,
then climbed into double-bottom darkness.

For hours he watched
the wandering arc's green glow,
accompanied by igniting sparks
spitting like long play fireworks.

Occasionally he snapped open
the metal lid of his Golden Virginia
and expertly rolled
an ever so slim cigarette

realising, once again,
a nightshift cat had done a piss.

And at dinner time
when he surfaced he rested his head
against a rusty pillow,

closed his eyelids and saw
the red glow of a summer sun
as weeds twined the stockyard pipes
and a Red Admiral fluttered past
accompanied by the drone of a honey bee.

The Difficulties of Discipline on the Football Field

The teams prepare for their daily game
eating dinner time pieces
and slugging cans of steaming hot tea
or having a sly nip from a half-bottle.

The teams
Twenty a side
ages sixteen to sixty.

The park
Stone cobbled pitch
criss-crossed railway lines
a skin of frozen snow.

The kit
boots –   steel toe-capped.
strip –   boiler-suits in various stages of decomposition.
tracksuit –   donkey jackets and overcoats
                 that have known grander occasions.
ball –   lifespan extremely short.

The ref
Everyone

The play
because of conditions underfoot
the teams moved in unison
as if the players' feet were interconnected
by a linking mechanism
like a Christmas toy football game.

The bevvy merchants
Under the illusion
they are keeping fit
as sweat beads their foreheads
before they have even kicked a ball.

The over-age players
relive past glories
thinking they can still show the young team
a trick or two
by feinting and weaving
and letting the ball do the work.

The young team
twist and turn and dummy and swerve and trap
and perform manoeuvres
which in their minds are majestic
and in reality are sometimes OK
and always likely to upset the opposition.

The conflict
of mad Shuggie McRitchie
who knows that his defence
must stand steady at all costs
as he stops Rab the caulker
with a chest-high steel toe-cap
that Rab takes exception to
and we know because Rab proceeds
to bounce a loose cobblestone
off of Rab's forehead

and the crimson stains the white

as the left winger slots home the winner
and continues his run towards the shed.

The final whistle
the twelve-thirty-seven horn
signals the resumption of building ships.

The Travelling Man from Northumberland

One night this guy
walks into the bar
orders up a pint of heavy
puts four matchsticks on the floor
in front of a chair
balances the pint
on the baldy top of his head
declaring he's cheeky Charlie from Northumberland
then proceeds to pick up each match
one
by
one
prior to standing on the chair
balancing on one leg
removing his jacket
putting a cigarette in his mouth
and lighting it with one of the matches
without spilling
one drop of the frothy beer
that is still perched on his baldy bit
then
beforewecandrawbreath
for his next trick
he caves in a penny
by pounding it

with the bottom of a tumbler
and informs us
he is just a travelling man
and rather than accept any of the drinks
he's being offered
he would prefer a coin or two
for the road
as we seven or so strangers applaud and cheer
on this Monday quiet evening.

Earning the Right

It was natural on Mondays

Jamieson would do little work –
as the DTs prepared him
for an evening of cold sweats and shivers.

On Tuesdays, Wednesdays and Thursdays
he would knock his pan in.

He would mark off and scribe and dab
and chop and guillotine and burn
and hammer and flange and roll
and chip and gouge and weld
and shape the reluctant steel plates
to whatever plans were given to him
as if his whole being depended on it.

On Fridays
he was two-speed
dead slow and stop

before going to the off-sales
for his dinner time carry-out
that made his overalls bulge
as he smuggled cans of Super Lager
past the gatehouse security

that he would down in the toilets
with his raised boots
keeping the cubicle door closed.

Later in the afternoon
the firewater taking effect
he would get uptight
because the foreman
continually clocked him
not working
not getting the fact that Jamieson
had earned the right
to prepare himself for another
weekend of serious swallying.

A Right Pain

If you were lying
on your toolbox at dinner time, dozing
he'd drip a bottle of brown sauce
into your open mouth.

And if you had
a brand spanking new pair of overalls
he'd rip off all the metal buttons, one by one,
just for a laugh you understand.

And if you were in the middle of a yawn,
you know, one that was really luxurious like –
he'd poke his finger
right into the centre of your mouth.

And if you were rushing in the morning
to clock in, just making the bell
you'd find that he'd poured a can of water
into the time clock card slot.

And if you were chewing the fat
with the older men who'd tell you

                    'You don't know you're living son,
                    see in ma day,
                    you'd hiv tae sweep the snaw
                    aff the plates in the morning
                    cause the sheds hid nae roofs'

sometimes he'd sidle up
with his concealed 'spiritual sky' joss stick
smouldering in his rule pocket –
and the men would sniff the air
and remark 'He's a nice enuff boay
but his heid's wasted wi they drugs.'

As I said... a right pain so he was.

Regulations

The cludgie attendant sits
officious

neatly folding
the regulation five sheets
of crinkly hard tissue paper

in readiness for the

click
click
clicking

of the regulation turnstile.

An overalled gentleman in metal swarfed overalls
leaves his clock number,
takes his tissues
and goes to the cubicle for a shite

that regulations state
should take no longer than seven minutes.

The Great Voltaire

The electrician
called himself the Great Voltaire
and worked at his bench
making up wiring harness after wiring harness
or in the ship's interior
feeding length upon length
of heavy cable
and, as always, would find time
for the homers of kettles, toasters and Hoovers.

At dinner time
he would down tools
then periodically yell

'Roll up, roll up, ladies and gentlemennnnnnnnnnn!'

and prepare himself
in the centre of the work area
where he'd crouch into a ball
as an assistant covered the magician
with a large upturned cardboard box.

From the box comes a muffled

Alacazam! Alacazim!

Then the assistant raises the box
to reveal
The Great Voltaire has dematerialised

and the boilersuited audience
whistle and clap and cheer
exclaiming
'Where the fuck has he disappeared to this time?'

The Great Voltaire
maintains his crouching position
and smiles...

knowing his magic
has once again done the trick.

The Little Drummer Boy

He played in the Renfrew Pipe Band
and would practise
in the fabrication shed
drumming with welding rods
on top of empty oil drums
like an exotic calypso performer
in the Mardi Gras in New Orleans
only he wasn't,
he was in the fabrication shed
in Clydebank
and had a crazed smile on his face.

His rat-tat-tat-tat-tatting being lost
in the daily cacophony
of whirring, screeching, grinding, hammering and clattering.

At home
he had a cloth apron
with a deep front pocket
in which was secreted a large cloth penis
attached to a string
attached to a can opener
and when a guest
asked for a can of pale ale to be opened ...

well, I don't have to spell it out.

At work
he'd take part in the dinner time football.
He was a wee tubby guy
past his best
but still had the moves.

The feint of the shoulder
and shuffle of the feet
and the backheeler
leaving the opposition hacking thin air.

Always the crazed smile on his face.

Black and White

In the Clydebank town hall
the right honourable member
rose to speak,
instantly receiving a thunderous ovation
from the overalled tradeunionists
in the body of the hall,
just as he was about to explain
the economic uncertainty of their industry.

And each time
he again tried to speak,
the applause and cheering got louder and louder.

And no matter how many times
his aides pleaded for order,
the cheering continued unabated
till he could take no more
and stormed out
leaving the unions with nothing
and no one to heckle.

The cheering stopped
and the hall filled
with a puzzled workforce uncertain
of what would happen next
until the welders' shop-steward
spotted the piano
on the stage beside
the right honourable member's
now empty chair.

And as he tinkled the ivories
with the hall humming along
in idle appreciation
a boiler shop labourer named Jazz
climbed on to the stage,
whispered into the steward's ear,
went up to the redundant microphone
and sang Billy Fury's 'Halfway to Paradise.'

The pianist theatrically rising to the occasion.

The following day
the newspapers reported.

The Right Honourable Member of Parliament
was forced to exit
because of his freedom of speech being violated
by an intimidating workforce
that bordered on the edge of mob rule.

The Dust Man

He broke off a length
of heavy-duty hack-saw blade.

He sharpened one end
on the grinding wheel
till through the flying sparks
the edge gleamed.

He wrapped coarse white-cloth-tape
round and round the other end
till his home-made handle
gave his home-made knife
the balance he required.

He climbed on to trestles
supported by wobbly planks,
and on his shoulder
he humphed his cardboard box
filled with insulation slabs.

He balanced on the planks
while he extracted the slabs
one at a time and fastened
them on to metal pins
welded to the duct's surface
that looked like a steel porcupine.

Then, like a master butcher
he cut slices of insulation
to clad the duct's metal skin.

And as his day wore on
the glass fibres floated silently
like small smoky snakes
into his atmosphere.

He opened his boiler suit,
pulled down his face mask
to relieve the sticky sweat feeling,
rolled a cigarette
and scratched the insides of his arms

and where the shafts
of sunlight filtered
through the galvanised shed walls
the dust particles
seemed at their most active
dancing their macabre dance.

On Being A Clerk

Tom was a fat man
tall and a bald head with beady eyes
he would rotate
in different directions at the same time
while saying
'I look at things this way.'

In the factory office
he'd play shoulder charges
hopping on one foot with arms folded
and maiming any other clerk crazy enough
to challenge him, the more wily opponents
swerving before impact
allowing Tom to crash into the metal lockers.

At dinner time he'd play chess
six challengers at a time
looking like mimics of Rodin's Thinker

and as they attacked his Sicilian defence
he countered, playing speed chess
moving like Billy Whizz
checking and mating
leaving the brains of the department
feeling as if they'd had
another intellectual boot in the balls.

A Few Swallies

In the inspection department
the men wore green overalls, yellow hard-hats,
carried clipboards and measuring tapes.

In their office
they smoked pipes
as if it were a Sherlock Holmes convention.

The new man
had recently been promoted
from the shop-floor
and found the monthly wage
impossible to manage.

He'd sit, surrounded by reports,
theodolites and dumpy levels
and, the week before payday

in among the smoky figures
he'd scoop up papers with both hands
throwing them into the air
like confetti at a wedding.

'I'm surrounded by complete incompetents,'
he'd shout at no one
crashing his fist on the desk top.

The others carried on puffing their pipes
recognising it was the end of the month
and things would look better for the new man
in the club at dinner time
after he'd had a few
swallies of the gabby-watter.

Phil The Fluter

At the Clydebank bus stop
Phil the Fluter
wore burst shoes,
a grey trench coat
and a trilby hat that had seen better days.

He performed
to the shuffling bus-queue audience
on his battered taped-up flute.

With 'Stranger on the Shore',
he serenaded his strangers
complete with his missing notes.

He scuffed past
each potential victim
playing his high-speed tune
before the next bus arrived.

To turned heads
he offered his upturned hat
for recognition rarely received.

The Nightshift Man

He downed a few halfs and half-pints
in the Seven Seas public bar.

His nightshift chaser
for the shipyard that never slept.

And inside the fabrication shed
dimly lit
like a Stanley Spencer cathedral,
the half-cut nightshift man,
Lilliputian against the funnels
that seemed to touch the shed's roof,
he shaped and formed the cold creaking steel.

And in between showers of spraying sparks
and blinding flashes of light

a fill of rattle hammer clatter screech and whine,

the nightshift man
played midnight darts,
munched three am makeshift meals,
and stole forty in cardboard box beds.

And when the job went wrong
he cursed long
into the wee small hours.

And in the mornings going home
to his bed he passed
newly risen nine-to-fivers
with faces as dreich
as the clouds above their heads
blotting out the blue of the sky.

First Aid

The ambulance man
in the first aid office
always put on a dod of cotton wool
Sellotaped over the wound no matter where it was.
Standard procedure.

We understood eyes were delicate
so, before the ambulance man
could do his worst

we'd do our own first aid.

When a piece of grit
got into an eye and it watered and burned
a boiler-suited colleague
would produce a manky handkerchief,
find a cleanish corner
twirl it to a point
with his spittled fingertips
and with one finger and thumb
spread the eyelids apart
and probe ever so delicately
with his home-made grit extractor
till the offending foreign body
was carefully removed
as if by a practised surgeon

leaving the ambulance man
with his cotton-wool and sellotape
still waiting for his next victim.

King Rat

Jazz was a hole-borer that knew
the last time the favourite
in the 2:30 at Musselburgh
had had a shite
and spent most of his time
studying form in the cludgie
or putting on lines with
Walter, the store-man bookie.

Jazz reckoned he was a semi-professional gambler.
Jazz worked all the hours God sent.

'Merr hours than the rats,'
was his catchphrase.

His favourite song?
'Two nights and a Sunday,'

and when there was an all-nighter on the go
at double time,
his grin would spread from ear to ear
as he laid out his flattened cardboard boxes
for his bed
and his rolled-up jumper
for his pillow
opposite the girlie pics
pinned to the sheet of plywood
that would be his headboard.

'A home from home,' he'd call it,
as his mind's eye imagined
seeing next week's wage-slip
with his eyeballs rolling round
like a fruit machine
just about to hit the jackpot.

Time Out

The apprentice turning journeyman
took the piss out of the men
by shouting out their names
and ducking behind machines
and smirking at the inquisitive
looks on their frowning faces
as they searched for the source of the sound.

He tack-welded the lids of their toolboxes.

He filled their jacket pockets with bolts.

He turned the juice up on their welding pots
so when they struck an arc
it exploded like an out-of-control firework.

He did this for four years
then his time was out
and it was the mens' turn
to initiate *him* in the ways of manhood.

They stripped the apprentice down to his Ys
and bound him with cloth tape
to a gas bottle trolley
and taped
a giant sculpted polystyrene dick
on him.

They then wheeled him
to the garment factory over the road
where the machinists were all women.
They left him there
on display
like a temporary art installation.
The women commented on his manhood.

They finally returned
to wheel their victim away
and when they crossed the road
they tied his trolley to a lamp post.

Leaving him to the heavens turning grey black
and cold rain mingling with warm tears
that trickled their way down
towards his
now sagging
polystyrene dick.

The Journeyman

Working piecework in the funnel shop,
building quick
but not quick enough,
lifting and hammering and cursing
because it takes too long
to wait on the craneman
who's looking after his pal
who stands him a few dinner time bevvies
at the Seven Seas public bar
and you know because
that's where you get your three-pint chaser
for your ashet pie supper
that you eat with your rusty fingers,
then you fall out with the timekeeper
because of the stupid time he put on the job
and you kid on the boy
who was daft enough
to let you put a brush handle
through the arms of his ovies
and you play spin the hammer
like it was your prize six-shooter
and you laugh when the boy tries it
and nearly breaks his toes
and you go to the burner
and patter him up
so he'll burn your job,
and you momentarily watch
his torch igniting

and the gas you couldn't see
exploding
like a bomb
and a cloud of rusty dust
and bodies hiding behind
guillotines and flangers and scrap buckets
and you squint through the haze
at the guy that's not there
because he's been blown down the passage
with a hole in his side
that he didn't have
before you pattered him up
and you stoat over to the first aider
who puts a dod of cotton wool
stuck on with Sellotape, over your eye,
and you realise how lucky you were
and how lucky the burner wasn't,
then again
he could've been the guy
that fell in the furnace,
the first aider wasn't much use to him,
neither he was.

Stopping Time

At 4.00pm the boilermakers
crowd clatty toilets.
They squirt jellied cleanser
on the black of their hands.

They nudge each other in the ribs
'Whit happened, did yi fa?'
Their standard *dirty hands* jibe.

At 4.10pm they fasten donkey jackets
and edge past oil-soaked machines
and the rumble of shed door rollers
into the blinding sun shining
on cobbled streets
behind massive closed gates
with barbed wire pelmets

joining
fitters, turners, joiners,
plumbers, sparks, labourers and all

and at 4.18pm
the shipyard's hooter's blast
punctures the quiet.

The gates are opened by the gateman,
a guard freeing inmates.
The human mass floods out
like a full time football crowd
spilling into pubs, trains, buses and clubs.

spilling into an escape that lasts

until the next morning's 7:30am hooter
when they shuffle their return.

Morale

The shop floor reckoned
the staff didn't know
their arses from their elbows.

The foremen reckoned
the next time the shopfloor
actually worked an eight-hour shift
would be the first time.

The shopfloor reckoned
Fridays were days reserved
for serious swallying.

The foremen reckoned
they knew all the shopfloor dodges
as that's where *they'd* come from.

The shopfloor reckoned
the managers couldn't manage
their hole in a barrel of fannies.

The foremen reckoned
they didn't know
if their arses were reamered or bored.

The nightshift reckoned
all crappy jobs
were left by the dayshift.

The dayshift reckoned
their night-shift colleagues had
grannies that were tradesmen.

And those that reckoned
they were key personnel
dwelled on their superior abilities

and understood
they were surrounded by complete incompetents

as morale plummeted to an all-time low.

The Shoogly Peg

The MD stood high on the gantry
like Caesar addressing his legions
and spoke solemnly
to the massed boilermakers below.

'Regretfully, the present economic climate
has necessitated management
having to establish
an initiative objective.'

'This will result
in a centralised refocused streamlining
of personnel infrastructure
allied with
an integrated resource forward planning schedule
based on
the company's global proactive synergy concept.'

And as he plundered
his buzzword phrase book
a wizened journeyman
noticed the puzzled look on
a younger colleague's face.

'It's like this son …
yir jaiket's oan a shoogly peg.'

Industrial Deafness

In the QUIET comfortable waiting room
of the private hospital

a guy comes through the door
exclaiming to his colleagues
that both eardrums are perforated,
his claim is looking good
and we murmur our approval,
we'll screw the bastards
out of every penny they've got
we think as we grow more deaf by the minute.

(And if all else fails
there's always bronchitis
        asthma
        vibration white finger
        or asbestosis.)

and I am acutely aware
it's too late to understand
the implications of

'Right enuff, wi thae big feet
yi could get a joab in the polis nae bother,
Ach, bit therr's nae need tae worry,
ah'll get yi a joab in the yards,
yi'll be fixed up fur life, so yi wull,
fixed up fur life.'

It's strange: in my head
I can still hear these words being said.

The Cloth Cap, The Bowler Hat, My Son and an Old Man

As I walked
round the museum exhibition
with my son

telling him stories
of my doing time in the 60s
and of how we went on strike
for the four year apprenticeship

He tried the hands on exhibits
        the welder's tongs
        the caulker's gun
        the steel wires twined into a steel sling

I explained the significance
of the cloth cap and the bowler hat
in the perspex display case

Then an old man sidled up to me
and told me that the men
who wore the bowler hats were buffoons
and even when they got rid on the bowler hats
they never got rid of the buffoons
and my son didn't look
but listened
as the old man confirmed his point
when he told me how
when the *Queen Elizabeth* 2 was launched
and the champagne bottle
didn't break the first time

the yard manager
put his shoulder to the ship
and started to push.

The Three Queens

In the display case
sit three queens.

Large scale models
that will never see
large scale oceans.

They have ...

> no buzz of passengers' cheering cheerios,
> no blasting horns piercing sea-salt air,
> no fluttering flags waving at winds,
> no propellers churning gloomy depths,
> > or screeching gulls
> > wheeling for tit-bits
> > discarded by the well-heeled.

Instead
their deserted decks
tower above
placards with chalked legend ...

Queen Mary (Hull 534)
A ghost ship eventually completed
by depression-hit, cloth-capped artisans.
A 30s' symbol of hope for the hopeless?

Queen Elizabeth (Hull 552)
A sister to meet the demand of the 40s
of weekly Atlantic crossings
by the likes of Churchill, Chaplin and Crosby.

Queen Elizabeth 2 (Hull 736)
The final Clyde-built liner
destined for a Caribbean old-age
due to the new fangled jet-planes of the 60s.

And all are surrounded
by appropriate memorabilia ...

       Faded launch cards at 15 shillings a seat.
       Cunard books of matches.
       Engraved crystal goblets.
       A propelling-pencil purchased on ship.

And, once held
by Queens Mary and Elizabeth,
a set of silver-handled scissors
decorated with silver seahorses

       no longer cutting silky ribbons,
       releasing bottles of bubbly
       to smash against hulls,
       their champagne froth
       dripping on to the greased slipways below.

Acknowledgements

Some of these poems have appeared in various forms in ...

Industrial Deafness	Crazy Day Press
Ergonomic Workstations & *Spinning Tea-Cans*	Taranis Books
Swiss Watches and the Ballroom *Dancer*	Taranis Books
The Shipbuilders	Birlinn Press
Mungo's Tongues	Mainstream Publishing
Drink the Green Fairy	Luath Press
100 Favourite Scottish Football *Poems*	Luath Press
The Old Man from Brooklyn *and The Charing Cross Carpet*	Mariscat Press
Septimus Pitt and the Grumbleoids	Luath Press

... a variety of magazines and anthologies including *Lines Review* and *West Coast Magazine*

... and also on the BBC Radio Ballads CD 'The Ballad of the Big Ships' and were performed at Glasgow's Royal Concert Hall as part of the 2007 Celtic Connections BBC performance, 'The Ballad of the Big Ships'.

Some other books published by **LUATH** PRESS

Scotland's Great Ships

Brian D. Osborne and Ronald Armstrong
ISBN 1 906307 04 0 HBK £25.00

We got close enough to touch the big ships that pass where the Clyde runs narrow and deep. We knew them all... They were OUR ships.
TOM GALLACHER

The Scots have a grand tradition of shipbuilding
going back thousands of years, from the Celtic birlinn to the *Cutty Sark* to her Majesty's Royal Yacht *Britannia*. During the 19th and the mid 20th centuries the Clyde became the greatest shipbuilding centre in the world, producing over 30,000 ships in 150 years and pioneering huge advances in marine engineering.

This book tells the tale of some of our most iconic ships, and in doing so captures the bustling world of the shipyards, the adventurous voyages of the exploration vessels and the race of sailing ships across the sea in the cut-throat business of the international tea trade.

Septimus Pitt and The Grumbleoids

Brian Whittingham and Mandy Sinclair
ISBN 1 905222 81 5 HBK £8.99

Enter the mysterious world of Septimus Pitt and The Grumbleoids, where colourful characters spring to life in playfully peculiar poems. Meet the new teacher with the bizarre
dress sense, and Mr Nobody, an unhappy spook who just wants to join the class. Find out the secrets of the retired puppeteer, and be scared – very scared – of the ghost of an ancient librarian and his faithful cat.

Drink the Green Fairy

Brian Whittingham
ISBN 1 84282 045 1 PBK £8.99

The last time I drank the Green Fairy was twenty-eight years ago on my stag night. I ended up upside-down, having been deposited in a rubbish bin with my legs sticking up in the air in Glasgow's Queen Street station.
BRIAN WHITTINGHAM

Brian Whittingham walks the streets of Glasgow, dips into people's lives and delves into the world of the Impressionist painters. The poems are quick snapshots, focusing on the particular of the ordinary and yet widening the gaze to the universal in life. Colour is not just splashed across the canvases of the painter's lives he explores, but finds its way into the lives of all those he encounters. With his own bold brush strokes Whittingham mixes the territories of high art and city streets, making both equally significant in the make-up of daily lives.

... the finest collection of poetry I've read in years.
DES DILLON

Details of these and other books published by Luath Press can be found at:
www.luath.co.uk

Luath Press Limited
committed to publishing well written books worth reading

LUATH PRESS takes its name from Robert Burns, whose little collie Luath (*Gael.*, swift or nimble) tripped up Jean Armour at a wedding and gave him the chance to speak to the woman who was to be his wife and the abiding love of his life. Burns called one of 'The Twa Dogs' Luath after Cuchullin's hunting dog in Ossian's *Fingal*. Luath Press was established in 1981 in the heart of Burns country, and is now based a few steps up the road from Burns' first lodgings on Edinburgh's Royal Mile.

Luath offers you distinctive writing with a hint of unexpected pleasures.

Most bookshops in the UK, the US, Canada, Australia, New Zealand and parts of Europe either carry our books in stock or can order them for you. To order direct from us, please send a £sterling cheque, postal order, international money order or your credit card details (number, address of cardholder and expiry date) to us at the address below. Please add post and packing as follows: UK – £1.00 per delivery address; overseas surface mail – £2.50 per delivery address; overseas airmail – £3.50 for the first book to each delivery address, plus £1.00 for each additional book by airmail to the same address. If your order is a gift, we will happily enclose your card or message at no extra charge.

Luath Press Limited
543/2 Castlehill
The Royal Mile
Edinburgh EH1 2ND
Scotland
Telephone: 0131 225 4326 (24 hours)
Fax: 0131 225 4324
email: sales@luath.co.uk
Website: www.luath.co.uk